FastForward™

Riffs, Licks & Tricks you can learn today!

Boogie Woogie Piano

with Bill Worrall

Riffs, Licks & Tricks
you can learn today!

FastForward™

Boogie Woogie Piano

with Bill Worrall

HAL•LEONARD®

Exclusive Distributors:
Hal Leonard
7777 West Bluemound Road,
Milwaukee, WI 53213
Email: info@halleonard.com

Hal Leonard Europe Limited
42 Wigmore Street,
Marylebone, London WIU 2 RY Email:
info@halleonardeurope.com

Hal Leonard Australia Pty.
Ltd. 4 Lentara Court, Cheltenham,
Victoria 9132, Australia
Email: info@halleonard.com.au

Order No.AM958925
ISBN 0-7119-8197-3

Written and arranged by Bill Worrall.
Music processed by Paul Ewers Music Design. Edited by Sorcha Armstrong.
Picture Research by Nikki Lloyd.
Artist photographs courtesy of Redferns.

Printed and bound in the EU.

www.halleonard.com

Introduction

Hello, and welcome to ▸▸**Fast*Forward***.

Congratulations on purchasing a product that will improve your playing and provide you with hours of pleasure. All the music in this book has been specially created by professional musicians to give you maximum value and enjoyment.

If you already know how to 'drive' your instrument, but you'd like to do a little customising, you've pulled in at the right place. We'll put you on the fast track to playing the kinds of riffs and patterns that today's professionals rely on. We'll provide you with a vocabulary of chord sequences and boogie riffs that you can apply in a wide variety of musical situations, with a special emphasis on giving you the techniques that will help you in a band situation.

▸▸**Fast*Forward*** *Boogie Woogie Piano* is an amazingly infectious piano style that we'll be explaining to you from basics to advanced techniques to show you how to become a foot-stomping boogie player par excellence.

We'll look at everything from scales and chords to glissandos and turnarounds, how to use intervals and phrasing, and we'll also give you a host of other tips for authentic boogie playing. If you've been playing for about 6 months to a year, can play comfortably with both hands together, and are familiar with some scales and chords, this is the book that will take you further. If you are a beginner or new to the piano, why not try a beginners method such as *Absolute Beginners* or *The Complete Piano Player* before moving on to this book.

All the music examples in this book come with full-band audio tracks so that you get your chance to join in. Practise and learn the examples and then take off on your own over the backing tracks!

All players and bands get their sounds and styles by drawing on the same basic building blocks. With **Fast*Forward*** you'll quickly learn these, and then be ready to use them to create your own style.

Tip

Look out for the tip boxes throughout this book. These will contain hints on technique, explanations of theory, and other useful information.

About Boogie Woogie

Long before radio, cinema, TV and the jukebox took their place in the American entertainment industry, the itinerant musician would liven up the weekends of workers in barrelhouses, honky tonks and cheap bars, spreading news, gossip and fun into their impoverished, tough and often short lives.
It is now a nearly a century since the birth of this new style but we need to look to the end of the 19th century for its roots. In New Orleans there was then, as is the case today, a melting pot of cultures including French, other Europeans, Creoles and African/Americans.

It was the fusion of two of the prevalent styles, ragtime and blues, which was to spawn what came to be known as Boogie Woogie. Ragtime was a major influence, but many composers like Joplin considered themselves to be serious musicians and insisted on the music being played note for note.

This was far too constricting for Blues influenced musicians however, who in most cases were self-taught, so they combined their earthy and untutored blues vocabulary to create Boogie Woogie.

Blues often has a much more melancholic character and emphasises personal suffering; Boogie Woogie on the other hand, despite sharing elements of the blues, is generally brighter, more vibrant and encourages a physical response such as dancing or hand clapping. Boogie Woogie is the Black American equivalent to White country hoe-downs – 'feel good music' that provided escapism from harsh realities of life.

What Is Boogie Woogie?

So much for its origins and social role – but what technically *is* 'Boogie Woogie'? Well, although it uses the 12-bar blues sequence for a major part of its repertoire, its most characteristic factor is the constantly repeated, hypnotic bass patterns (ostinato) played with endless and infectious vitality, topped off with the sparkling riffs and runs in the right hand. The vocal, blues harp (harmonica) and guitar influences are also evident in the crushed notes, which try to emulate the bends and slides found in the Blues.

The good news is, that although Boogie Woogie can get very complicated, the right hand (melodic) part can actually work very effectively with just a couple of notes (check out the jazz classic 'C Jam Blues' for a later example of this).

JOOLS HOLLAND

Chapter 1: Three-Note Boogie

Left Hand Riff

This piece is designed to illustrate just how little you can play and still make a valuable contribution to the band. It's worth remembering that although as a soloist it may be impressive to play frenetic and flashy pieces within a band, for Boogie Woogie it is often the case that less is definitely more!

Our first example shows how easy this can be. The right hand part is made up of a simple three-note motif (a figure or short riff). In fact, if you left out the F♯ grace note at the beginning of the bar, you would literally be using just two notes in the right hand. This type of repeated right hand figure is a classic example of boogie piano and one of the mainstays of boogie playing. The left hand part spells out the essential harmonies that make up the 12-bar sequence.

Despite its simplicity, if you were to play it note for note with your local band while the guitar soloed on top, you'd certainly be doing enough.

Adding Basic Chords

This next example uses the same very simple left hand part and introduces the basic chords or harmonies of the 12-bar blues sequence. First of all, look at the chord chart below. It shows the harmony changes of the basic 12-bar in the key of C major.

Another useful trick is to memorise the pattern of the three chords that make up the 12-bar. As you're going to be using it for a large part of your boogie playing, you'll be happier and more confident when you can feel the sequence, instead of having to read each bar.

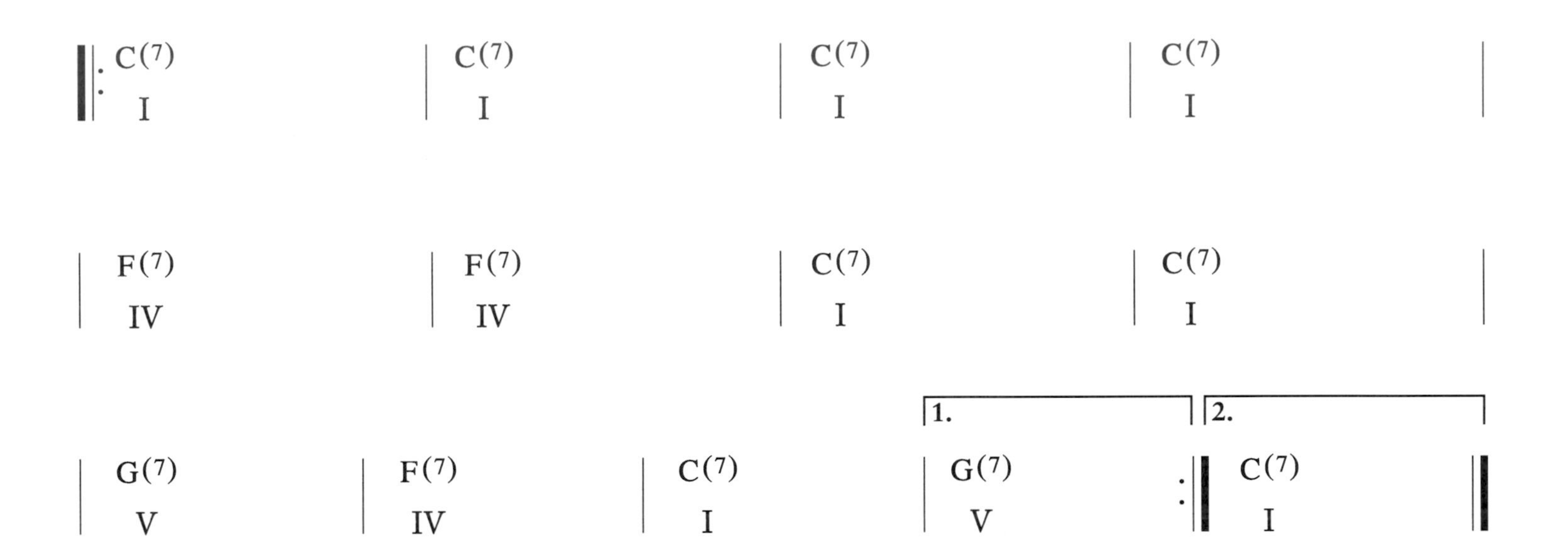

12-Bar Lyrics

The 12-bar is inseparable from the blues, and forms a substantial part of the boogie repertoire. In its most simple form it uses three chords (I–IV–V) and consists of three four-bar sections. Usually the melody (and the words if there are any in section one), are repeated in the second section, the interest being supplied by the harmonic change.

Finally, and as it was often ad-libbed, the singer was given a chance to think of a last line, to round it off, e.g:

My baby's gone left me
Oh she's gone left me all alone
My baby's gone left me
Oh she's gone left me all alone
I'm feeling tired of waiting
Wond'ring if she's coming home.

Adding a 'Turnaround'

We've put a 'turnaround' at the end of this example. You have two options – either stay with G and go back to the beginning, or go to C and end. Watch out for another common feature of boogie piano: the grace note. These are used by the pianist as a means of emulating the pitch bends that pretty much every other member of the band can do.

Grace notes are literally crushed into the chord and you can sprinkle them almost anywhere, but if you'd rather leave them out until you're really comfortable with the basic chords, it will still work fine.

Left Hand Boogie Pattern

Here we introduce what is one of the simplest versions of a boogie left hand pattern. Like the right hand part it is made up of three notes: in this case the root, 5th and 6th of the scale of C. These are then transposed (moved up and down in exactly the same shape), to continue the harmonic sequence.

Although you've already played the right hand part in the first example, make sure the bass is really solid before trying them together, especially as you're playing triplets with the right hand, and swung quavers with the left. Listen carefully to Track 5 if you're in doubt as to how to play this.

Pedal

The term 'pedal' originated in organ music of the baroque period when a note was played on the pedal and held while the harmonies above it changed. You could also have a 'pedal' sustained part in the middle or, as in our example, invert it and put it at the top.

Right Hand Melody

You'll have noticed while playing the first two pieces that the right hand plays the same notes throughout, irrespective of the harmonies. This is known as an 'inverted pedal' in classical music theory.

This is a fundamental and essential technique in Boogie and rock, but there are other occasions where you'll want to use different notes to spell out the harmony changes, and we'll look at those later.

So, have a go at this next example, first on your own, then with the backing track on CD.

TRACKS 5+6

Left and Right Hand Patterns

This next example puts together two patterns in the right and left hand, which you have already learnt in previous examples. You could practise the parts separately, and then put them together when you feel more confident.

TRACKS 7+8

As with all of the examples you should practise each hand separately until they are really tight and secure and only then begin playing them together. If you've studied classical piano, you'll already be familiar with the process of practising hands separately.

This technique is equally important in Boogie Woogie, but as you have the band to play along with, it needn't be boring either. It's a good idea to use the backing track to practise one hand at a time: it will keep you in time and, naturally, you'll sound a *lot* better!

Grace Notes and Slides

Here's a chance for you to practise your grace notes or slides, but this time we're playing over different inversions of the chord. Listen carefully to the chord as it moves up and down, and try experimenting with your own variations. In this example the slides often occur on the middle note of the chord, but try playing them on the top and bottom for some different sounds.

When sliding from a black to a white note you'd normally use the same finger. Obviously when going the other way it's not possible and you're more likely to get more articulation using separate fingers. Experiment to find the most comfortable way for you. Also look out for the turnaround in bar 12, which uses a 'chromatic shift' in the left hand from F, to F♯, to G. We'll look more at turnarounds later.

Passing Chords and Syncopation

Here, we introduce two new elements: passing chords, and syncopation. One of the most common passing chords – and the one we're using here – is a 4th above the main harmony, or 'F' on 'C' (bars 1, 3, 7, 11). There's also a passing chord in bar 5: the B♭ (in the harmony of F).

Notice that in bar 1, we're playing a C7 harmony, which works even though the third of the chord (E) is missing.

Also, at the end of bar 1, we use a device called 'anticipation' – here, we're playing a chord and holding it over the barline. This creates a much more syncopated sound. Try playing it on the downbeat of bar 2 and feel the difference.

MEADE LUX LEWIS

Chapter 2: Getting Even

Duple Time

In Chapter 1 we used a bounced or shuffle pattern (known as compound time) as the underlying rhythm for our pieces. Now we are going to use the other main rhythmic foundation of western music, called 'duple time', where the principal beats are divided evenly.

Even or Bounced?

Although occasionally boogie-woogie melodies will have odd sub-divisions such as 5 or 7, generally the main pulse or left hand base will be either even (duple) or bounced (compound).

Left Hand Pattern

So let's 'get even'. As in Chapter 1, the left hand starts with an alternating octave pattern but as you're now playing quavers (eighth notes), it's immediately got more drive to it.

Right Hand Pattern

The right hand uses another classic device, which is 'approaching' or pre-empting the basic harmony with the chord a fourth above (IV - I) or alternatively a tone above (II -I).

Chord Progression

A quick look at these two chords, (G and Em in our present example of D major), and you'll see there's only one note different between them. They obviously sound similar and, equally importantly, they have a similar harmonic role. This is another example where boogie has influenced pop / rock piano. Check out *Billy Joel's* 'My Life' – one of many classic examples of left hand octave parts.

Have a go at this, and then play along on your own with the backing track!

Glissando

If you need a bit of instant gratification or just a rest from reading, try a *glissando*. Just put your right hand thumb anywhere near the top of the keyboard, plonk it down fairly hard and slide down the keys to the bass end. It's that simple! So next time you get to bar 13, join the band and get glissing!

TRACKS 13+14

Adding Grace Notes

Here, we're simply adding grace notes to the right-hand part of the previous example, giving it more of a blues feel. You should practise these grace notes until they become a natural part of your playing and you can throw them in at will.

As in Chapter 1, I personally prefer adding the grace notes in the middle of the chord, but try experimenting with the other possibilities and see which works best for you.

Pentatonic Figure

Now we'll introduce a few more variations. Notice the little figure at the end of bar 4. The last two notes (the B to the D) use an interval from the pentatonic scale, which is commonly used in Boogie Woogie, as well as blues and rock. It makes a slightly more 'rounded off' sounding phrase.

Also, the left hand 'pedal' pattern stops at Bar 12. This is simply so that you can show off the flashy right hand riff – and hopefully the rest of the band will stop too and indulge in your moment of glory!

TRACKS 17+18

Right Hand Riff

Next, we introduce a short riff which is a bit like the grace notes we've already come across, except that it uses three 'grace notes' before the final note. These are to be played in a triplet: if you're not sure of the rhythm of the triplet, listen to the example on the CD.

You'll notice the pattern has also changed in the left hand, to include more of the 'walking bass' you previously played only at the end of an example. Here, it's being used throughout the example – and it gives the piece more of a driving rhythm.

Listen to the CD and then have a go yourself over the backing track.

Left Hand Boogie Pattern

You've already worked on the right hand part, so now we're going to introduce a traditional left hand boogie pattern. As you can see, it's a simple, repeating short riff. Once you've got the hang of the rhythm, it's just a matter of transposing the whole pattern up to the IV or V of the key chord.

The trick is to practise the left hand until you can do it with your eyes closed: then you can let yourself think about the right hand. If you try to do both together at once you may end up in knots!

As before, practise slowly and then speed up so you can join in with the band.

Put It All Together

In this last example, we'll combine different melodic elements from previous examples over our new boogie bass to create a more complete piece. Pretty much all of the melodic material is interchangeable so try out some different combinations and then, most importantly, work out some variations of your own.

Chapter 3: Gumbo Groove

It's time to head south to the state of Louisiana. We've already mentioned that the original boogie patterns emerged from New Orleans, but many variations have developed since then. The most famous boogie left hand patterns are the driving figures, but there are other boogie bass parts which are more laid back, funky and rhythmically fragmented. These are exemplified by players like Professor Longhair, Alan Toussaint and Dr. John: colourful names and definitely colourful music!

The basic left hand groove pushes strongly into the third beat using the F♯, which gives it a real kick and a completely different feel and colour from our earlier pieces. As before, it's mostly repetitive, so once you've got the hang of the basic rhythm, you can concentrate on the right hand.

The right hand uses a bluesy interval known as a 'tritone' (the notes B♭ and E) which, over the C in the left hand, almost makes up a chord of C7 – a very common Blues and Boogie chord. This right hand part is slightly more challenging – but take it easy to start with and you'll soon be playing along with the band!

More Bass Movement

In the next example we've added some more movement in the bass which you may find useful to keep the momentum going when playing by yourself, particularly when you come up with your own melodic ideas.

Notice the little '8' underneath the bass clef: this denotes that all the notes shown should be played an octave lower.

7th Chords and Tritones

In the last two examples, we came across the beginnings of 7th chords, and the use of intervals known as 'tritones'. The 'tritone' is basically an interval made up of two notes which are exactly three tones apart. It can be played anywhere, but when used with certain notes or chords, as in the example above, it can create a '7th' chord.

The thing to remember with 7th chords is that the 7th note of the scale is actually a flattened 7, so in C, it would be B♭. That's how a tritone of B♭ and E, over a bassline of C, can create a C7 chord, even though the 5th of the chord (G) is missing.

The 7th chord is a very commonly used chord in Boogie Woogie and also in Blues and Jazz. Look out for it in the next examples!

▶▶ HENRY GRAY

'Stop' Turnaround

The next example uses the same basic groove but this time, we've added a turnaround with a stop on bar 11, which ends with a definite finish in bar 12. We've seen the stop, or break, before in Chapter 2, but in this example the break is for two bars instead of one, and ends the piece rather than taking it back to the top again. Harmonically a subtle variant is heard in bar 5, where there is now the outline of an F9 chord with a G in the middle, in place of the previous A. This creates a softer sound than the tritone.

TRACKS 29+30

Adding a Melodic Line

Now we're familiar with the bass pattern, let's add a melodic line. So far, we haven't looked at scales or modes in any detail, so let's investigate the next example.

Opening Harmony

As our opening harmony is C7, the traditional leading note 'B' is replaced by a 'B♭', and the only occurrence of the 'B' would be as a passing note between B♭ and C. So we now have an F major scale – or a scale of C with a flattened 7th.

Added to this we have an F♯ (♯4) which functions as a grace note, resolving onto the dominant 'G'.

Finally, we have an E♭, also functioning as a grace note, rising to the E. It occurs as part of the C7 harmony, injecting the tune with a blues feel.

Chromaticism

Although the harmonic basis of boogie is diatonic (i.e. based on the major scale), melodically it generally uses more chromaticism than in the 12-bar blues we are using as the basis for most of our pieces.

Scale Change

In more simple diatonic music, where there is little or no chromaticism, you may well be able to use the same scale (melodic material) for the entire piece. But because of our use of successive flattened 7th chords, we need to change the scale to fit the harmony. In bar 5 when the chord changes from C-F, we simply transpose the opening scale up by a 4th.

This doesn't mean we have to use all of the notes however, and in this case the only addition is the A♭ (♭3), but hopefully this spells out your options.

TRACKS 31+32

Exploiting The 7th

To further illustrate the interchangeability of our various components, in the next example we have combined the melodic line from the last example with the turnaround from the one before.

Dissonance

In boogie we often use the flattened 7th (e.g C7), and more potent 'dissonance' (e.g. 9th, 13th, etc) on successive harmonies. But a few centuries ago, when harmony was developing, the interval of the 7th (most frequently on the dominant) was viewed with some distaste.

To lessen this offence, the offending note would be 'prepared' by playing it in the previous harmony, in which it was consonant, and then repeating it in the dominant 7th chord. E.g. playing an 'F' as part of a D minor chord, then repeating the same 'F' as part of a G7 chord (see below). Well, today pretty much anything goes, but if you ever want to keep the transition between harmonies really smooth, it's quite a useful tool.

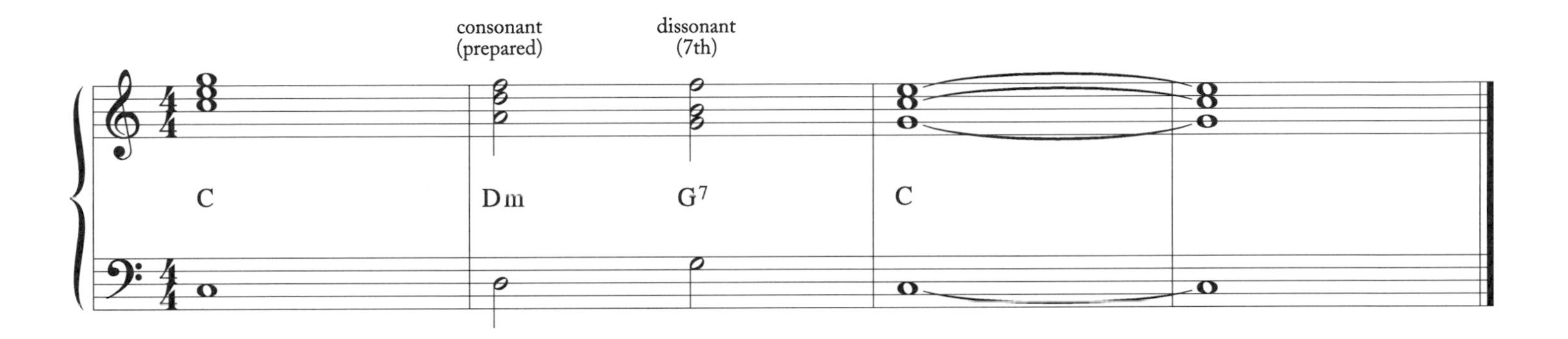

DR JOHN

'Gumbo Boogie'

In order to give you a bit more to play, we've doubled the length of the last example in this chapter. The two basic left and right hand ideas have been combined, and there are some additions in the second half. This is a good example of how you'd play with a band as part of a whole piece.

In the first chorus you're playing the groove, either to establish it at the beginning or as the harmony part while someone else plays the tune, and in the second chorus you take over the melody. As I've said, there's a bit more to do in the second half, and this is due to the intervals of 6ths and 3rds that have been added to the tune. You'll probably find the thirds easier to begin with, but the piece will work if you just play the top line, so add the lower parts whenever you feel comfortable.

TRACKS 35+36

Chapter 4: Broken Bass

In this chapter we're going to look at another fragmented/ broken bass pattern, but instead of accenting the third beat as we did in Chapter 3, we now don't play it at all! To illustrate these new possibilities, a grace note has been added to the bass part that anticipates beat 3 on every other bar. You could use it on every bar, or, if you want to keep it simple, leave it out to begin with.

Although it's a simple device, it makes the bass part feel like a two bar pattern – and generally the longer the phrase you can create or imply, the better. Anyway, it's time to wallow in those southern flavours once again as we look at another piece of Cajun extraction.

▸▸ KEITH EMERSON

Arpeggiated Passing Chords

In this first example, the right hand uses passing chords on bar 2, which we've already seen, but this time they are arpeggiated. Rhythmically, we use the same pattern for the first two beats of bar 1 as in Chapter 3, but the effect is completely different due to the different bass line, and the fact that it's an open chord (root and fifth) instead of the previous tritone. Check out the differences and listen to some of the examples in Chapter 1 to compare.

Reduced Bass Line

A simplified bass line is used in this next example so that you can concentrate on the right hand. There will always be exceptions to the rule, but study the direction of the melody as influenced by the chords.

At the beginning the A♭ functions like a grace note, rising to the A on the F harmony (minor 3rd – major 3rd), but when we change to the B♭7 chord, the A♭ (now the 7th) falls.

Four-Note Boogie

We keep the reduced bass line for this example and add a different melody that simply uses the first four notes of the scale. The whole pattern is then transposed up a 4th for the B♭ harmony and back down again at bar 7.

On the dominant (C7) we go chromatically up from the 3rd to the 5th, and in bar 10 we do a little dance around the 3rd. Finally, there is another stop at bars 11 and 12 for the turnaround.

Syncopated Bass Line

Here, we use a new, more syncopated bass part, which features grace notes. Spend a little time on this – then move on to the melody. It's similar to the one in the second example, but you'll notice a little more embellishment in bars 7 and 8, and in the turnaround.

Here's a good opportunity for you to do some improvising: base your melodies around the harmonies we've been working with in this chapter – and the basic 12-bar blues pattern – and you should have no problems with this!

Add It Together

Here, you're simply combining the bass line from the last example, with the melody from the third example in this chapter. Watch out for bars 7, 8 and 11.

TRACKS 45+46

Solo Intro

In this last piece we come to one of my favourite figures, and although it will work just fine within the tune with the whole band playing, it's a pretty sure bet everyone will have a smile on their face when you kick off the number by yourself.

As with all the other pieces you can break this intro down into smaller parts, learning one bar at a time.

You'll notice a tremolo, or 'shake', at the end of bar 4 - ignore how it's written and simply practise alternating between the C and E♭ as quickly as you can. Tremolos are an essential part of your boogie repertoire and, unless you have a sudden stop at the end, you can bet you'll be using a tremolo or a glissando to finish most of your tunes.

Chapter 5: Rock 'n' Roll

Show Off

We're going to move on to the rock 'n' roll end of boogie for this chapter, but we'll still be able to use a lot of the same melodic and figurative ideas and patterns.

The right hand goes back to using the tritone and the left hand uses an octave pattern while we get comfortable with the faster tempo. Watch out for the 6ths in bar 9: if you find them tricky, just play the upper part until you're able to play them with ease.

TRACKS 49+50

Using The 6th

Another use of 6ths is shown in the next two examples, so before we go on to use them in a 12-bar, lets see how they're constructed.

If you take out the first note (D♯) of the first group of three, you'll see we're just using two notes from the scale of 'C'. If we add the first note again it should be obvious that this is like a leading note or pickup into the following 6th.

In this first example the first note is always a semitone below the following note, which means it is sometimes a chromatic note or one that isn't in the C7 (F major) scale.

This tends to give it a more honky-tonk feel but try it with diatonic notes only, and you should be able to hear the difference.

Rhythmic Variation

This example shows one rhythmic variation of the previous one, but try to find some of your own. When starting on the black notes you may find it easier to use the index finger going to the thumb (2-1-5) and when starting on the white notes use the obvious 1-2-5 fingering.

6ths and 7ths

In this example, we try using the descending '6th' figure we just learned, over a C7 harmony. The left hand simply pedals on C for the first four bars, so you should be able to concentrate on the right hand part.

TRACKS 53+54

Moving Bass Line

The next example introduces a new bass line to which we add our tritone right hand from the first example in this chapter (page 44).

The left hand pattern has long been a Boogie favourite: it has a lot of character but feels easier to play, and more upbeat, than some of the other patterns.

TRACKS 55+56

11th Chord Harmonies

The last example uses a stabbing C11, which you might usually hear being played by the horns as a backing figure. The 11th chord has a more contemporary and less bluesy feel to it, but it's a useful chord to add to your repertoire.

Chapter 6: Turnaround Blues

The Turnaround

So far, we've tried some simple turnarounds at the end of the 12-bar sequence, but now we're going to try some variations at the beginning to kick it off. The opening sequence in the first example is very well-known and you'll probably recognise it if you've ever been to a blues gig or concert.

In this slow bluesy style, the use of 'walking tenths' is a common device, being a form of stride piano playing. There may be many of you who are unable to reach a tenth, and although you can split them to make it easier, we're going to use thirds in the left hand for the first few examples. They aren't nearly as powerful as the tenths, but hopefully they'll give you an idea of the effect.

We'll also look at the pentatonic scale. We've used elements of it in previous numbers but this is the first example where we use it exclusively to construct our melody. As is probably obvious, the pentatonic scale consists of five notes: 1, 2, 3, 5 and 6 of the major scale, and although you may feel it somewhat limiting, it does have a unique character. As a basis for a tune, riff, or solo, it is ideal material. As with all rules or conventions in scales, learn them, use them and when you're ready, break or change them.

Below is an example of a pentatonic scale, ascending and descending, in G.

G pentatonic

Pentatonics

The pentatonic scale is one of the most-used scales in blues and rock music. Its versatility makes it the ideal scale to use when soloing over changing chord progressions. It's also used as the basis for many riffs and melodies. Make sure you know this scale!

TRACKS 59+60

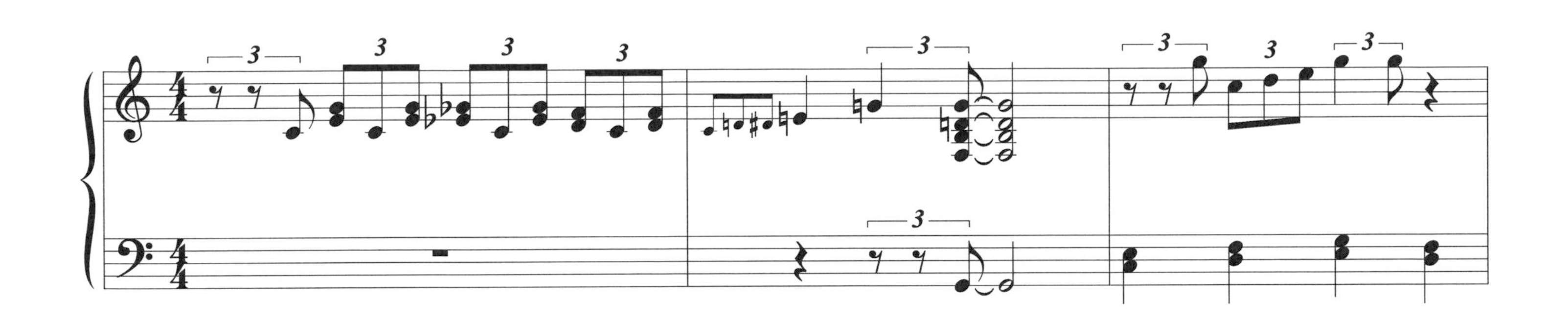
3
3
3
3
3
3
3
3
3

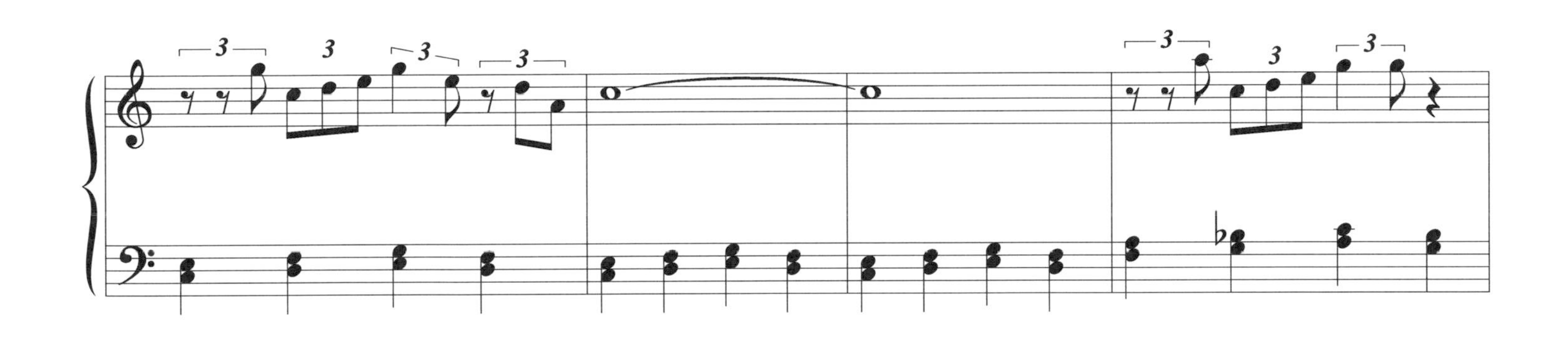
3
3
3
3
3
3
3

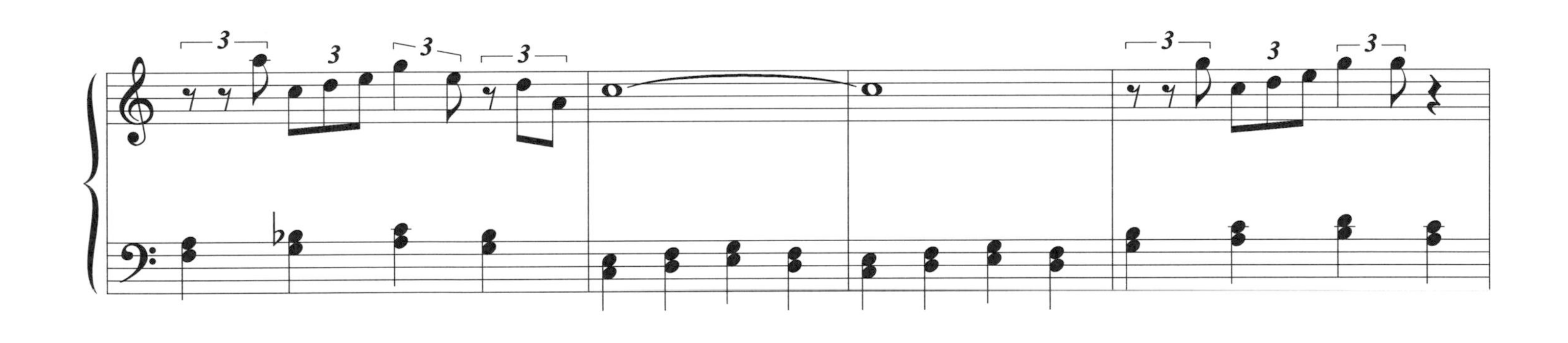
3
3
3
3
3
3
3

3
3
3
3
3
3
3
3

Harmonic Change

The next example uses some more variations on the turnaround and melody. Four bars from the end of the sequence, there is a harmonic change where, instead of the normal dominant ('G'), we have a chord of 'D' (still a key chord: it's II minor in C).

Broken Octave Pattern

The next example uses some further variations on the turnaround and the melody departs from the pentatonic scale with the addition of B♭, E♭ and F, but because of its construction, the pentatonic influence is still obvious. The left hand introduces a broken octave pattern which changes the feel again, but the thirds from the last example will work equally well if you prefer them.

Left Hand Tenths

Another small variation in our turnaround starts the next example, and at last the tenths we've been working towards. If you don't want your wrist aching all night don't try this for too long and don't worry about leaving the odd one out, some tenths feel – and are – bigger than others!

As mentioned earlier, you could split the tenth, playing the lower note first and then immediately skipping up to the higher one. This is a good preparation for stride piano (see the example below) where the bass note is followed on the next beat by a chord.

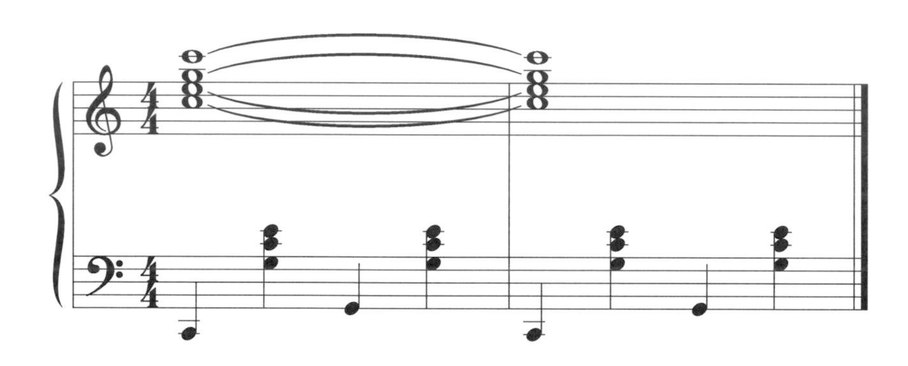

ALBERT AMMONS AND PETE JOHNSON

TRACKS 65+66

Turnaround Variation

We have a final variation in our turnaround for our last example, followed by a new melody which departs further from the pentatonic scale and uses more of our earlier melodic influences. On the dominant chord at the end of the turnaround, a different type of that chord has been used, to show you some of the possibilities you can use. Look out for the tremolo in bar 11!

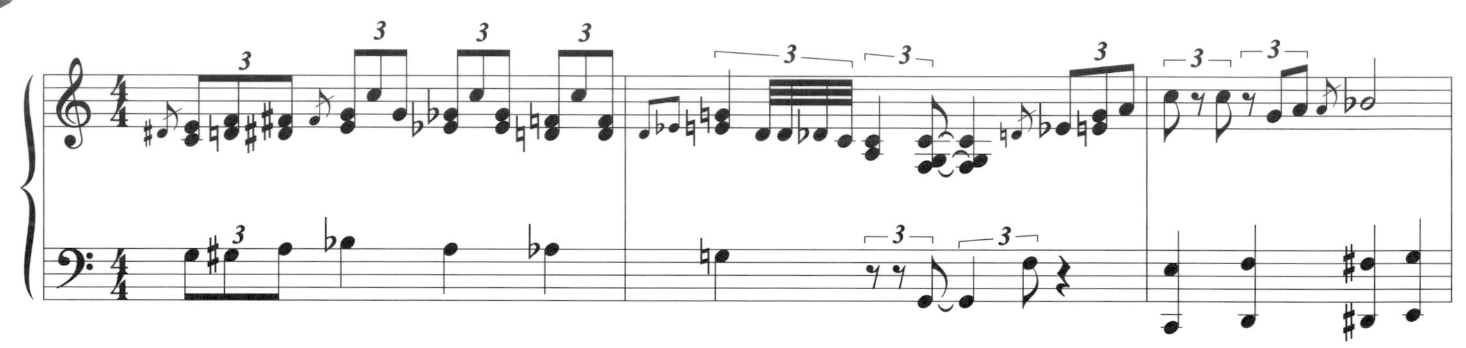

Pick-Up Bar

So far everything has been in a straight 4/4 rhythm, but you might prefer some of the turnarounds starting with a pick-up on beat 4. The following bar now has one beat less, so becomes a 3/4 bar. See the example below to see what it would look like written this way:

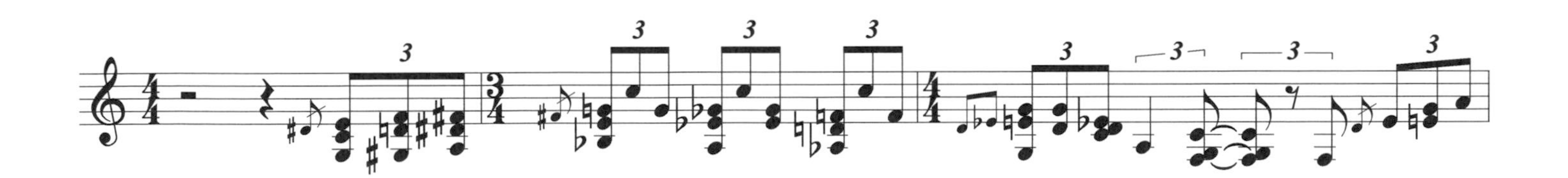

JELLY ROLL MORTON

"New Orleans was the stomping ground for all the greatest pianists in the country."

Chapter 7: Break Stop Boogie

We start the final chapter with a stop or break section in the first example (4 bars). These stop bars also function differently, as they are part of the 12-bar sequence and not pick-up bars.

Although we haven't used it so far, another harmonic variation in the 12-bar sequence is the use of the IV chord (subdominant) in bar 2. The voicing used here is essentially a C9 – but try playing a straight C7 to hear the difference. The bass line that we're starting with is a simple arpeggio on the three chords I-IV-V. What you should be aiming for is a part that is interesting, but not so complicated that it gets in the way when you are in this supporting role.

TRACKS 69+70

We've looked at some three-note figures and how they might be started on different beats of the bar to syncopate the rhythm, and I'd like to explore that further.

If you take any three-note figure and play the notes as bounced *or* even eighth notes, it will take you three bars before you get back to your starting note on the down beat (see below).

You can break this cycle at any point, and here are a few of the possibilities using this device. Whilst we're thinking in threes, I've also introduced some quarter note (crotchet) triplets so you can work on your syncopation.

TRACKS 72+73

The next example starts with a six-note figure, which, if repeated over and over in 4/4, produces a syncopated pattern. As before, you can break this cycle at any point, but to illustrate its effect over a longer period from bar 5 of the sequence I've used a three-note figure and kept it going for seven bars. Notice that it crosses all the harmony changes, which adds to the syncopated effect.

This example also uses a bounced rhythm, but would work equally well with even eighth notes (quavers).

Finally, to keep the left hand busy, the last example adds an alternating octave pattern to the left hand arpeggio. This moves around more than the other bass parts, so don't be surprised if you find it tough to start with. And when you're ready, add the right hand part you just learned in the previous example.

Conclusion

Congratulations on reaching the end of this book! Hopefully your boogie playing has come on in leaps and bounds, but there's an awful lot more out there than we've had space to cover, so don't put your feet up just yet. We've also covered a lot of theory which hopefully you've found informative and useful, but it's worth remembering that most of the boogie legends probably knew very little theory, so don't worry if you've skipped over some of it. The most important thing is to get stuck in with the band and enjoy playing!

JOOLS HOLLAND

Further Reading

If you'd like to continue improving your piano or keyboard playing, why not check out some of these great books, available from all good music retailers or bookshops. In case of difficulty contact Music Sales Limited (see page 4). You can also visit our website: www.musicsales.com.

FastForward 12-Bar Blues Piano
AM92445
Discover the blues with this book and CD pack. Includes basic blues structures and techniques, original blues to jazz and rock piano, boogie, stride and walking bass styles.

FastForward Real Blues For Keyboard
AM92438
Learn to play the 12-bar blues using authentic techniques, to get the real blues sound. Play along with the CD, and discover how bands get their sound.

Chord Encyclopaedias
The essential source books for all piano and keyboard players. 384 blues chords and 480 jazz chords in standard notation, plus keyboard diagrams, for instant note recognition.
The Encyclopaedia Of Blues Chords AM92592
The Encyclopaedia Of Jazz Chords AM92591

Barrelhouse and Boogie Piano
OK64659
Transcriptions of 22 original solos from some of the boogie piano greats: Jelly Roll Morton, Memphis Slim, Meade Lux Lewis and more.

Dr. John Teaches New Orleans Piano
Vol.1 HSB00699090
Vol.2 HSB00699093
Vol.3 HSB00699094
Learn how to play authentic boogie woogie straight from one of the legends. Dr. John explains licks, turnarounds, tenths, right-hand fills, parallel fifths, and a host of other essential boogie techniques.

Jelly Roll Morton: The Piano Rolls
AM960300
Original artists' transcriptions from 1920's piano rolls. Includes 'King Porter Stomp' and 'London Blues'.